BURN ThIS BOOK

... and Move On
with Your Life

BURN This BOOK

... and Move On with Your Life

Jessica Hurley

**Andrews McMeel
Publishing**

Kansas City

02 03 04 05 06 RR2 10 9 8 7 6 5 4 3 2 1

ISBN: 0-7407-2699-4

Book design by Holly Camerlinck

Burn This Book has been printed on recycled paper.

A becker&mayer! book, Bellevue, Washington.
www.beckermayer.com

Attention: Schools and Businesses

Andrews McMeel books are available at quantity discounts
with bulk purchase for educational, business, or sales
promotional use. For information, please write to: Special Sales
Department, Andrews McMeel Publishing, 4520 Main Street,
Kansas City, Missouri 64111.

To Mom:
For learning which things to let go of and for
making room for positive change

Acknowledgments

I'd like to thank Jean Lucas and her cohorts at Andrews McMeel Publishing; Ben Raker, Suzanne De Galan, and the rest of the hardworking crew at becker&mayer!; Christopher Pease for his insight into ritual and myth; my Campalicious, New Melones, and KBHK posses; my former coworkers at ThriveOnline who bravely let go of their amazing award-winning Web site (on healthy living), and learned to start anew; Gary Evans, an inspirational leader; Lynn, for showing me the ropes; Judy, for keeping me sane; Dr. Nadler, for sharing "heavy and down"; my dad for his puns and my mother for her "psychobabble"; and the rest of my supersupportive family, roommates, friends, and Tika—for just being there.

Renewal Through Fire

He knows his time is out! and doth provide
New principles of life; herbs he brings dried
From the hot hills, and with rich spices frames
A Pile shall burn, and Hatch him with his flames . . .

—Claudian, *The Phoenix* (circa A.D. 4)

Throughout history, cultures and religions around the
world have used elaborate fire rituals to symbolize release,
rebirth, forgiveness, and cleansing. Buddhists use fire rituals in meditation to clear the mind of the negative effects
of human passions, which are thought to hinder one's
attainment of enlightenment. Some cultures use fire to
banish evil spirits while others feed sacred flames with
offerings that rise heavenward in plumes of smoke and
sparks. For some, a fire ritual takes the form of a tiny
candle set silently afloat in a lantern on a moonlit river;
for others it is a roaring, tribal bonfire, complete with
drumming, chanting, and dance.

In the Western world, scorned lovers often toss letters
and reminders of "old flames" into a fireplace to signify

the end of a relationship and, frequently, the beginning of a new chapter in their lives. Several countries mark holidays expressing hopes and resolutions for new beginnings—independence days or new years—with brilliant pyrotechnic displays.

Regardless of the scale of the flame or the relative solemnity of the ritual moment, there is a sense shared by all that the act of burning can be a liberating form of release and purification—one that provides a path toward starting anew.

Meanwhile, most of us carry around emotional baggage without realizing how it affects the quality of our everyday lives. Do you have trouble letting go of past mistakes? Do you internalize resentments or continue to blame your parents for the way you were raised? Are you still pining away for the great love of your life you lost many years back?

We grasp on to these types of detrimental experiences and feelings because we often find comfort in the past, like old security blankets. We seek forgiveness for our own mistakes—but, in many cases, find it is easier to blame other people than take responsibility for our own actions. Sometimes, our pride blocks the way to forgiveness. We think that protecting our egos will prevent us from being rejected in the future. Unfortunately, the reality is that, if not released, such feelings tend to snowball—taking on more power and keeping us from living joyfully.

So how do we rid ourselves of the negativity that

seems to shadow us? We take action! Oftentimes we're controlled by what we're not aware of; we must first take notice of things that bind us—patterns or behaviors that hold us back in life, things we want to change. Being conscious of these challenges will empower us to map out new paths. One of the most effective ways of gaining a new perspective on problems, and simultaneously working to correct them, is to mark the event and decision with a symbolic cleansing gesture, such as a fire ritual.

This book offers a uniquely active and involved reading experience—one in which symbolic destruction brings mental rejuvenation. It offers renewal through one of the oldest means available—the eternal element of *fire!* Contained here are suggestions for releasing unhealthy behaviors and emotions. Tear out the pages that resonate with your circumstances. Internalize the simple lessons, and then put them to the flame. Cast them one by one into a fireplace or campfire or set them ablaze individually with the strike of a match (in a fireproof container, of course). As not everyone faces the same challenges, blank pages at the back of the book allow you to create personalized letting-go rituals. Burn this book and send your plaguing thoughts and bad habits up in smoke.

Like the mythical phoenix after the fire, your spirit is free to rise from the ashes to new heights once you've cleansed the negative emotions and behaviors from your life. And just like the fiery sun, which is extinguished by nightfall and reborn with each day, a new dawn awaits you!

I will no longer blame my parents for my choices.

As long as you continue to blame others for your choices and mistakes, you'll be playing the role of a victim—a role in which you are likely to feel powerless over your own life. The first steps toward empowering yourself are to take full responsibility for your actions and to learn to forgive your parents for the mistakes they made. Keep in mind that they are only human and may be playing out patterns passed down from their own mothers and fathers or clinging to societal expectations.

You are capable of replacing negative familial cycles with positive ones by making a conscious effort to do so. As an adult, you have the power to select which lessons and values from your upbringing to embrace and which to discard. You can and will make decisions that are good for you, regardless of your past.

I won't let self-doubt get the best of me.

Do you have a running dialogue inside your head that tells you that you aren't good enough or that you're sure to fail? Don't let this damaging inner voice prevent you from accepting challenges or appreciating your accomplishments. Combat this self-defeating behavior by infusing your thoughts with positive words and phrases and surrounding yourself with supportive friends and family. You have many wonderful attributes, and the more you build upon them, the less powerful your self-doubting side will become. Make the choice to be your own strongest advocate, not your own worst critic. Imagine negative words such as "can't" and "bad" dissipating in the flames.

I will let go of the need to be perfect.

Face the facts now—you will never be perfect! The good news is that nobody else will be, either. Expecting yourself and others to meet such lofty goals will leave you tired, anxious, and frustrated. Instead, learn how to go easier on yourself and find a happy medium, where you'll really understand the meaning of "good enough."

What would really happen if you didn't balance your checkbook to the penny? Probably nothing. Perfect people are not only obnoxious, they also exist only in TV Land, where dishes don't have spots and you can create a beautiful table centerpiece in "just minutes," made from dust bunnies and an old shoelace.

Instead of focusing on all of the areas in which you think you fall short, spend time celebrating your imperfections and the idiosyncrasies of those around you—these are the characteristics that make us each unique!

5

I will break habits that are harmful to my health.

Do you resolve to quit smoking each and every New Year's Eve? How many times have you told yourself that you'll start getting more exercise? Think of the things you could do right now to improve your health and well-being. Then, throw your bad habits into the flames once and for all and replace them with positive patterns and activities that enhance the quality of your life.

I will remove unhealthy friendships from my life.

Almost everyone has an acquaintance who is an emotional vampire. She might be the neighbor who is always asking for "just one more favor." He could be the friend who is always in crisis, but is nowhere to be found when you need a shoulder to cry on. These are the people who suck up your time and energy and give very little in return. Perhaps you continue giving to them because you feel guilty or have trouble setting boundaries.

Get rid of these people, and while you're at it, you also want to give "harshmellows" the heave. When you're feeling happy and relaxed, the harshmellows are the people who ruin your mellow mood by stressing you out or bringing you down.

Pay special attention to the relationships in your life and figure out which ones are healthy and reciprocal. Then, gradually start weeding out the interactions that bleed you dry. If you truly value a friendship, try to work it out with the person before cutting it off. Remember, there are plenty of amazing, caring individuals in the world—so take time out to enjoy the warmth of the great people you know.

I will bid adieu to an unrequited love.

Do you continue to have romantic longings for "the one who got away" or the one who was never yours in the first place? Holding on to these type of relationships often prevents us from being open to meeting and having successful unions with new people. It's time to relinquish your hopes that one day you'll get back together and live happily ever after, because these thoughts stop you from living in the present.

This doesn't mean you need to completely forget about the emotions you held for a loved one. You can keep these feelings in a special place in your heart, while still deciding to move on to new, exciting chapters in your life. It may be a cliché, but it's oh-so-true—when one door closes, another opens . . . and you never know who just might walk in.

I will free myself from my fears.

Fear can be a good or a bad thing, depending on how, when, and where the emotion is utilized. It can be the motivating force in a situation of "fight or flight." For example, if a bear were chasing you, fear would give your body a big shot of adrenaline so that you could elude the grizzly creature.

Unfortunately, more often than not, people are afraid of all that is unknown, thus fearing life itself. You might be scared to attempt a career change or fearful of taking trips by yourself. These forms of fear stop us from getting the most out of our lives and prevent us from making changes for the better. They can also keep us from expressing ourselves fully because we're afraid others might not approve of our opinions or will reject us.

It's time to assess your fears and determine whether they are helpful or harmful to your overall well-being. Cast the anxieties that impede your success into the fire and start embracing the intoxicating mysteries of this world.

I will negate my need to control.

Are you a "control freak"? Many of us respond to a chaotic world by standing rigid and trying to maintain a sense of control, even though feeling like we have complete control over anything is only an illusion. We can make choices and take actions that contribute to a specific outcome. However, no matter how well prepared we are, "happenstance" can and will occur, and most of the time we'll never be able to accurately predict what form it will take.

What happens when we are rigid and inflexible? Just ask activist Julia Butterfly Hill, who lived for more than two years in a redwood tree to protect a forest from a lumber company. During storms, the turgid tree branches were the first to snap off, while those that could bend and move with the winds survived. She had to learn to do the same.

Those of us who resist the constant changes and the seemingly chaotic nature of life will face the most pressure. This idea, which is prevalent in Buddhism, shows how life is in a state of constant flux and those who accept it and can "go with the flow" are apt to experience the most contentment. So loosen up, let things go, and let things flow. Isn't it time you made more room in your life for serendipity?

I will cut loose unhealthy attachments.

Buddhists believe that unhealthy attachments and desires keep humans from attaining enlightenment. Nirvana and enlightenment might be a tall order, but that doesn't mean you can't look at the ways in which your attachments to people and material items might be hindering your happiness.

In our culture, we often get caught up in the obsession to obtain more and more. "Having enough" always seems to elude us.

The less attachment you have to objects, the less likely you will be to get upset if your favorite sweater gets lost or your new sports car gets a dent. Things come and go. People come and go. It is the cycle of life. The same goes for expectations. If you aren't tethered to a specific outcome, you are less likely to be disappointed, and you'll leave yourself open to be pleasantly surprised. That which you hold, holds you, so let go and be free!

I will stop getting burned by love.

It is next to impossible to avoid at least one broken heart in a lifetime, but you can eliminate patterns in which you are constantly getting burned by love. So many of us fall into traps of loving someone who isn't capable of returning our affection. We put ourselves down and think that if we were only "good enough," the object of our desires would care the way we do.

It's time to stop this cycle of thought. If you don't feel good enough, then you are likely to attract someone who isn't good enough for you. Don't let fear or neediness keep you in a bad relationship. You deserve someone who will treat you right and appreciate you for the amazing person you are.

I will cast my pride aside.

Pride can be a good attribute or a bad one depending on how it's manifested. If you've worked hard, it's good to feel pride in your accomplishments. However, pride can also keep loved ones apart, and it can stop someone who really needs help from reaching out.

When appropriate, cast your stubbornness aside and forgive that someone you have been holding a grudge against. Carrying all those negative feelings around isn't doing anyone any good. Next, learn how to forgive your-self. We all make mistakes, and all you can do is learn from them.

I will say sayonara to stress.

Like good fear, good stress can motivate you to accomplish great things. Bad stress, on the other hand, can be dangerous to your health, your relationships, and your psyche. Take a good hard look at your life and pinpoint the things that make you the most anxious. Is it money? Your boss? Your significant other? Figure out what you need to change for a more relaxed lifestyle.

It helps if you schedule plenty of time between appointments so that you have time to breathe and collect yourself a bit. Learning to step back and take long deep breaths is a great way to lower anxiety levels, as are meditation and yoga practices. Try this little mantra: *I will face stressful situations with grace and integrity*. Now, find out what stress-busting method works best for you.

I'll make a bonfire of my vanities.

Do you spend more time and money on your looks than you do in creating a rich inner life? While it feels good to look good, don't place too much importance on your appearance and how you'd like others to perceive you. Not only are vain people a bore, but personality is a much wiser long-term investment. As you age, your spirit is what shines through when your youthful glow has diminished. Practice humility—it's only human, and so are you.

What other ways might you be self-centered? In conversations, do you spend too much time talking about yourself instead of listening to others? Do you demand all the attention in groups or are you confident enough to let somebody else take the spotlight? Strangely enough, vanity is oftentimes a sign of insecurity, so in order to give your inflated ego the heave-ho, you might have to work on self-esteem. Go ahead, enter your own "inner-beauty" pageant!

I will stop being careless about the environment.

Too many people use "one person can't make a difference" as an excuse for how we treat the environment. We consume so much every day without thinking about how products were created and where they will be disposed of once we're through with them that we are running out of resources, our landfills are maxed out, and we're polluting this planet at an alarming rate.

The first thing you can do is take responsibility for your own actions and consumer choices. Remember, you have consumer power and every penny spent is a vote for your beliefs. Throw out your bad habits and replace them with the 5-R mantra: Respect, Rethink, Reduce, Reuse, and Recycle. Then, demand that larger corporations and politicians take accountability for their environmental atrocities. Stand up and show everyone that one person can, and will, make a difference!

I will put off procrastination.

When you have a big project due, how often do you find ways to do everything but what needs to get done? Do you leave it until the last minute—until the stress monster is breathing down your neck? Do you look for distractions or tell yourself that you will get to the project once you have all the other little things you need to do out of the way?

When we procrastinate, we not only make ourselves more anxious, but oftentimes our work suffers because we don't leave sufficient time to get things done. Consider this great metaphor for time management: Think of a bowl as your time and various sized rocks as the things you need to fit into your schedule. If you put in the pebbles (representing your smaller tasks) in first, you will notice that the larger stones (your larger tasks) are more difficult to fit in. If you place the big rocks in first, the smaller pebbles easily slide between the crevices and everything fits in the container. It's not too late to turn over a new leaf.

I will not live my life with regrets.

You've heard the clichés "No use crying over spilt milk" and "Hindsight is 20/20." People often wonder what might have happened if they had done things differently or taken another path. "I should have taken that job." "I should have told him I was sorry." We chastise ourselves with what we think we should have done or said in a given situation. The truth is a waste of energy to lament over past things you cannot change.

This does not mean that looking at past "mistakes" can't be used to your benefit. If you come upon a similar circumstance you can learn from your experiences and apply your newfound knowledge. Take notice of your "errors," and then let them go.

It's important to remember that in many instances, one option is not necessarily the "right" one and the other the "wrong" one. Life isn't usually so black and white, and often-times what first appears to be "bad" turns out to be "good." For example, you'd probably be happy you missed your flight if the plane ended up making an emergency landing. Unless you have a crystal ball, you can't possibly predict the reverberating results of each action. Send your shouldas, couldas, and wouldas packing, and enjoy the present of presence.

I will resist the urge to please at the expense of my own needs.

Has someone ever asked you what you wanted to do, and you responded, "I don't care. Whatever you want to do"? How are others going to get to know you if you're only showing them a reflection of their wants and desires? Ironically, people pleasers who try to make others happy at the expense of their own needs often find themselves in a losing battle. Instead of being popular, others walk all over these martyrs and find them to be displeasing.

In order to gain others' respect, you need to show respect for yourself and your needs and set personal boundaries (and, most important, keep them). Instead of exerting all of that energy on other people, redirect it toward yourself. Loving yourself isn't an easy task, but you can start off by taking more time for yourself and asking others for what *you* want from them for a change.

I will let go of my need to prove myself to others.

When you look to others for your self-esteem, it's like anchoring your ship onto a sandbar. Accept it now: You really can't please all the people all the time; you're lucky if you can please only a few people, part of the time.

We often think we're putting all of the pressure on ourselves, when actually we're responding to messages that our society, family, or friends have sent us. It can be tricky to rediscover what you want instead of what others want for you. As each of our fingerprints are unique, so are our wants, desires, and lifestyles.

If you try to fit someone else's mold, you're likely to look in the mirror one day and not recognize your reflection. (This is one of the reasons people have midlife crises.) Remember, even the good-natured Dalai Lama has some people who don't like what he does. Save the molds for Jell-O, and let your spirit be free to choose its own glorious shape.

I will replace prejudice with compassion.

We are all judgmental to a certain degree, but some are more judgmental or have more prejudices than others. If you have unwavering opinions about what is "right" and "wrong" and what is "good" and "bad," it's easy to misjudge others and alienate yourself. Practicing compassion is a great way to break the chains of closed-minded thinking.

Instead of jumping to a negative conclusion about someone, try to put yourself in her shoes. A woman once ran through a red light and crashed into my car. She was obviously upset, and she couldn't believe that I wasn't yelling obscenities at her for causing the accident. I wasn't angry with her, because I thought about how I'd feel if I'd done the same thing. The woman felt bad enough, and rubbing salt in her wounds wouldn't undo what had been done. Additionally, if you know that others have stereotypes about you, break free from them and demonstrate just how multidimensional you really are.

I will not let jealousy get the best of me.

Many a murder has taken place as a result of lethal doses of love and jealousy. This combination can turn a fairly normal person into a raving lunatic. Jealous feelings might cause you to ruminate for hours on scandalous scenarios you've manufactured in your mind: You might call your beloved many times a day just to check up on him or her. If you find a mysterious phone number in your sweetie's coat, you assume it's from a lover, not the repair place down the street. A little jealousy can be healthy, but these are all indicators that it's going too far.

Combat this demanding emotion with self-esteem and trust. If you're not feeling good about yourself, it's easy to project that your honey might be looking for someone "better." Secondly, if jealousy is interfering with your relationship, you have an issue with trust. Has your mate done something in the past that gives you reason to doubt his or her fidelity? If so, this needs to be resolved with your significant other, or you may need to find greener pastures. As they say, "trust is the foundation of a healthy relationship."

I will reject my fears of rejection.

Sometimes you just have to take the leap,
and build your wings on the way down.
—Kobi Yamada

Do you avoid pursuing your dreams because you are afraid of failure? Do you suppress your feelings because you are fearful of rejection? Do you have abandonment or intimacy issues that prevent you from having healthy relationships? Well, it's time to unpack your emotional baggage and send it to the junkyard. Don't let your insecurities run your life and keep you from living up to your potential. Take that leap of faith, and share your gifts with the world!

I will choose not to participate in idle gossip.

When you stick your nose into someone else's business, somebody's feelings are bound to get hurt. Negative things you say may get back to the subject of the gossip, or that person may just walk in and catch you off-guard. Also, I know too many people who have traded scandalous information via e-mail and accidentally sent the message to the person they were gabbing about (oops!).

When talking behind someone's back, you may end up losing that friendship. Those to whom you tattle may not trust you with their own news. Think twice before you pass information through the grapevine, or the subject of your friends' gossip might turn to you! And when negative rumors come your way, neutralize them with the power of kind words.

I will stop anger before it reaches the boiling point.

Anger, like many other emotions, can be used constructively, though that isn't usually the case. It's a great way for humans to protect themselves against bodily harm. If channeled correctly, it can also be used to spark passion for a good cause.

Unfortunately, when kept inside, anger can lead to resentment, high blood pressure, and heart disease. And, outwardly expressed fits of rage can be psychologically damaging to others and may lead to acts of violence.

When your blood begins to boil, step back and take some deep breaths. You may need to take a walk or even see a counselor if you can't seem to get your anger under control. It can be helpful to remember the difference between aggressiveness and assertiveness. When you are assertive, you can stand up for your beliefs without being intimidating. Aggressive behaviors just put others on the defensive. Most important, focus your attention on the things you have in common with another instead of where you don't see eye to eye. Choose your battles wisely. If all else fails, agree to disagree.

I will stop playing the role of the victim.

Have you ever known someone who is always complaining about their life, yet doesn't do anything to change it? Or a friend who always seems to be the victim of some unfortunate event? If you are victimized once, that's one thing, but when it seems to be a recurrent theme in your life, you need to take a closer look.

When we are filled with self-pity and point our fingers at others in blame, we often put a big label on our foreheads that says VICTIM. To break this negative cycle and empower ourselves, we need to take responsibility for the role we've played in this cycle. Maybe you have chosen to surround yourself with untrustworthy people. Perhaps you haven't been taking good care of your health, so you get sick.

Don't blame someone or something else and call yourself a victim. If you have experienced more than your share of unfortunate events, call yourself a survivor, because that's what you are!

I will deny denial.

In this day and age, there are so many methods for escaping emotional issues that a person could feasibly live in denial for her entire life. TV, movies, video games, liquor, drugs, sleep, sex, and work can all be used as distractions to avoid looking closely at yourself and your life. Some people are so ashamed about things they've done that they can block out entire events or completely change the story in their minds. And they actually believe it.

To combat denial, take time to meditate or walk by yourself each day (without headphones). In the quiet, listen to any nagging voices that you've stuffed in the back of your subconscious. Even if the issues are difficult to face, you will experience much more emotional pain if you try to avoid them. Denial ain't just a river in Egypt, you know!

I will reduce the number of buts and ors in my life.

Are you down to earth or is your head in the clouds? Are you naughty or are you nice? Are you wrong or are you right? Unfortunately our culture isn't very comfortable with paradoxes. Most people feel like they must be one thing *or* another, which leads to confusion. We live in a colorful world, so it doesn't make sense to make everything black or white. Don't limit yourself.

My grandma Miriam always says that the beauty in life comes from the ANDS. You can be down to earth *and* have your head in the clouds. You can be both naughty *and* nice. You can even be a psychologist *and* a go-go dancer. Likewise, you can lose your *buts* without quitting smoking or spending hours on an exercise machine. The ways we often use the word "but" is the same way we use "or." It is exclusionary. For example, instead of saying "I like your art project, *but* I think it could use more blue," say "I like your art project, *and* I think it could use more blue." Discover the peace of mind that comes from accepting the *ands* in life.

I will reject the need to conform.

Physically, emotionally, intellectually, and spiritually, we all come in many shapes and sizes. It's no wonder we get so bent out of shape when we try to squeeze ourselves into someone else's mold. Even if your mother, your spouse, or the latest magazine thinks they know better, only you know what's the right fit for you. Invent your own definitions of success instead of conforming to someone else's ideals. Individuality is a custom fit. Accept no imitations or limitations!

I will ignore impatience.

We are impatient with ourselves, as well as with other people and things. We kick ourselves when it takes us a long time to figure out a problem. We kick the computer when an Internet page takes too long to load. We snap at others when they don't do things as quickly as we want them to. Many people also curse the ways in which things move too slowly in other countries. We should learn to appreciate the fact that in many other cultures you don't need to always be in a hurry—take the time to relax and smell the flowers.

We also don't have patience with the universe in letting things come to us in their own due time. As kids, when taking trips, we would bug our parents incessantly with "When are we going to get there?" As adults, we aren't much better—we subconsciously do the same thing on a much grander scale. We say to ourselves, "I'll do that when I get out of college, when I get that job, when I have kids, when I have more money, or when I retire." We often forget to enjoy the journey, because we are too impatient. Instead, we focus on the destination. Don't fret about the future; take the time to be present in the now. Be conscious and aware of all your senses. Remember, it's not the end result that's important, it's what you learned along the journey to get there that counts. Take it slow, and enjoy each moment on the path of life.

I will knock down the walls that separate me from others.

Have you put up an impenetrable wall around yourself so that you won't feel vulnerable? Unfortunately, this defense mechanism may do more harm than good. Barriers may keep people out, but they can also keep you locked inside a fortress of loneliness.

Pretending to be a tough person on the outside is usually just a method to protect a soft heart. Turtle shells and porcupine quills keep the bodies of the creatures safe, but would you want to snuggle up with one? Probably not. Unless you want to live a life of solitude, create at least one door in your hard exterior. This way you will leave yourself open to the experiences of being fully alive.

I will not lose perspective on my concerns.

Very few people haven't blown a problem out of proportion at one time or another. However, some of us are masters at creating mountains out of molehills. We can easily lose perspective on the actual size of an issue.

To prevent concerns from snowballing, discuss what's on your mind with a trusted friend or confidant to gain an objective view. Also, remind yourself that the subject of your worries will probably mean nothing to you years, or even days, from now.

Other ways to get a grip on the actual magnitude of your life's circumstances is to spend time with children and elderly people or use nature as your teacher. You'll be amazed at the lessons you'll learn from watching an ant colony or sitting under the stars. You'll see how your concerns measure up in this vast universe. Remember, you may be small, but your small part is important.

I will cast off worries about the future.

My grandma Arlene used to tell me that worrying was a waste of my time because, in her experience, the things that did happen she couldn't have imagined in her wildest dreams. Many people (especially "control freaks") are under the illusion that fretting is the same thing as preparation. Well, it's not.

Worrying about something without taking action is not only a waste of energy, it can also be harmful to your health and your psyche. If there is no action you can take, faith is your best ally: faith that you have the skills to handle whatever comes your way and faith in the universe that everything will work itself out. It's like the Serenity Prayer says, "Grant me the serenity to accept the things I cannot change, the courage to change the things I can, and the wisdom to know the difference."

I will clear my clutter.

In feng shui, the clutter in your environment can lead to mental clutter, which makes it challenging to have a clear outlook. The practitioners of this ancient art form believe that the placement of objects in a space can obstruct or enhance the movement of energy or chi.

Start bulldozing your way through the excess piles of junk in your home, car, and office. Set up simple systems to keep your paperwork organized. Clean out your closets and donate the stuff you never use to charity or hold a garage sale. With all the new space you'll create, you'll have more room in your life for positive and clear thought.

I will weed out wicked words from my vocabulary.

Pay closer attention to the words that you use and the effect they have on others. Negative things you say in haste may stick with someone for a lifetime. I know a woman who spent a lifetime covering up her beauty with excessive makeup, simply because when she was a young girl someone mentioned that she looked like a boy. Whenever she looked in the mirror, this very feminine woman continued to see the face of that boy.

If you have a sharp tongue, remember that most people don't enjoy hanging out with someone who is constantly critical or pessimistic. It's also important to listen to the ways you talk about yourself. If you say things like "I'm such a dummy" or "I'm too fat," your self-esteem can suffer or others may make the mistake that you're actually fishing for compliments. Instead of planting the seeds of negativity, discover the bounty that is produced when you cultivate a respectful, positive vocabulary.

I will not ignore my intuition.

How many times have you ignored the little voice in your head or the feeling in your gut that tells you to do something? Later, you kick yourself because you didn't listen to that little voice. We often blow off our intuition because we have trouble trusting something that seems so abstract. When making decisions we tend to place the emphasis on our intellect instead of our hearts.

It's not crazy to have faith in intuition because your body, spirit, and subconscious are gathering information all the time, even if you're not aware of it. During meditation or a quiet walk, zero in on what your higher self may be trying to tell you. Use the messages you receive to help you fulfill your deepest desires.

I will unload my information overload.

We are barraged with so much information and technology each and every day, it's amazing that we can even hear ourselves think. It's hard to know what we really feel when so many messages and metamessages are telling us how to act, how to dress, and what kind of car to buy.

Make a new resolution to cut down on the amount of TV you watch, news stories you read, and Web sites you surf—at least for a little while. I mean, do you really need to know who Julia Roberts is dating now or get up-to-the-minute reports on bowling trends? Consume information consciously. Investigate different sources to find the select few that meet your needs. After unburdening your brain, use the space you've freed up to concentrate on the things that really matter to you.

I will replace codependency with interdependency.

Codependency has become a catchphrase throughout the Western world. How do you know if you or someone you love is codependent? Determine if the person is using a relationship to avoid facing his or her own issues and taking accountability for them. Someone who gets their sense of self-worth from constantly taking care of others instead of themselves would fit the bill. ("I didn't know I was codependent, I just thought I was being nice.") So would those who constantly let others take care of them so they don't have to face challenges on their own.

If a person is constantly negative and full of self-pity, would you feel bad about yourself if you can't make them feel better? Now, imagine if someone vomited on the street. Would you go and try to pick up the puke? Of course not! Don't pick up someone else's issues just so they don't have to own up to them.

On the other hand, interdependency is a good thing. It feels healthy. Everybody wins. People are accountable for themselves and their actions, and they work as a team. It's the central force behind a healthy community.

I will let go of the need to do it all.

We play so many roles in our daily lives that we often feel we can't handle the load. You might be the parent, the employee, the maid, the accountant, the artist, the lover, the landlord, the nurse, the yogi, the student, and the teacher all in one.

The truth is, the more things you do, the more the quality of some of the tasks will suffer. As a friend once told me, "You can't do it all without taking the dings." Assess what matters most to you and prioritize accordingly. Maybe you'll let the house get a little messy so you'll have time for yoga. Maybe you won't have time to go to the gym, but you will get exercise playing with your kids instead. At the end of each day, forget about what still needs to be done and give yourself a gold star for all that you've accomplished!

I will temper envy with appreciation.

Are you seething with envy whenever you watch a show about the lifestyles of the rich and famous? Do you wish you could be more creative like your older sister or have a car like your neighbor? Get over it!

Envy may give you a clearer picture of the goals you desire, but it can leave you feeling discontented, always reaching for the dangling "carrot" just out of your grasp. Remember that movie stars and the likes have tons of publicists and makeup artists to make their lives look glamorous. Instead of buying into this "manufactured reality," try placing more emphasis on appreciating the things you already have.

I will root out the sources of my depression.

Millions of people live with depression, yet they never seek treatment because they're embarrassed—afraid to let others know that they are less than perfect. If you suffer from depression, first look at what your feelings might be trying to tell you. Deep sadness can often be a sign that you aren't living your life in congruence with your desires and values. The only way to solve this sort of situation is to take action and make changes, even if they are scary.

If you aren't able to get a handle on your downward spiral, contact a professional who has training in this field. If you don't like the first person you go to, keep looking until you find a good fit. Think of a therapist as a personal assistant who helps you make the most out of your life. Remember, you truly deserve to be happy.

I will . . .

_____

_____

_____

_____

_____

_____

_____

_____

_____

_____

_____

_____

_____

_____

I will . . .

_____

_____

_____

_____

_____

_____

_____

_____

_____

_____

_____

_____

_____

I will . . .

_____

_____

_____

_____

_____

_____

_____

_____

_____

_____

_____

_____

_____

_____

_____

I will . . .

_____

_____

_____

_____

_____

_____

_____

_____

_____

_____

_____

_____

_____

_____

I will . . .

_____

_____

_____

_____

_____

_____

_____

_____

_____

_____

_____

_____

_____

_____

I will . . .

I will . . .

_____

_____

_____

_____

_____

_____

_____

_____

_____

_____

_____

_____

_____

_____

I will . . .

_____

_____

_____

_____

_____

_____

_____

_____

_____

_____

_____

_____

_____

I will . . .

_____

_____

_____

_____

_____

_____

_____

_____

_____

_____

_____

_____

_____

_____

Suggested Reading

Let Your Worries Go by Jessica Hurley

52 Relaxing Rituals by Lynn Gordon and Jessica Hurley

52 Ways to Stay Young at Heart by Lynn Gordon and Jessica Hurley

Don't Sweat the Small Stuff by Richard Carlson, Ph.D.

The Language of Letting Go by Melody Beattie

All I Really Needed to Know I Learned in Kindergarten by Robert Fulghum

Wishcraft: How to Get What You Really Want by Barbara Sher

Creating a Charmed Life by Victoria Moran

The Art of Happiness by His Holiness the Dalai Lama